A Dragonfly Will Do

A Dragonfly Will Do

True love is about looking forward,

together, into eternity.

Beverly Quin Jones

XULON PRESS

Xulon Press
2301 Lucien Way #415
Maitland, FL 32751
407.339.4217
www.xulonpress.com

Printed in the United States of America.

ISBN: 9781545613344

Note to Reader

A mother's worst nightmare came true for me on March 14, 2003. My only child died in an accident. This book is for those who have experienced the loss of a loved one, a painful event, or a tragic circumstance and are struggling to cope with their loss and grief. This book is a compilation of "short stories" from the journals I kept over a fourteen-year time span. Through these "stories" , I hope you will see and understand how I learned to live with loss and grew to experience a full life of peace, hope, and joy.

Life for me did not follow the plan I wanted, but it is what I got, so I had to make a choice. I did not know what my future held, but I knew who held it. I chose to surrender my pain and my life to God. I remembered a saying my mother had hanging in her kitchen: "There is nothing that can happen today that God and

I together can't handle." Day by day and with "eyes of faith," I focused on His Presence. I experienced God's love and grace all around me through nature, through my friends and family, and through reading His Word.

Corrie ten Boom, who suffered in a Nazi death camp, has a profound quote about the power of focus. She says, " If you look at the world, you will be distressed. If you look within, you will be depressed, but if you look at Christ, you'll be at rest."

TABLE OF CONTENTS

"Mom, I'm Going Home!"

It was 3:00 A.M. Suddenly, I was awakened by a voice. The voice said only four words. The voice said, " Mom, I'm going home." I recognized that voice. It was the voice of my 26- year- old son Brandon, and I knew exactly what he meant. I was startled, and I was scared. Was I dreaming? It sounded as if he were standing right behind me delivering that message. The words were powerful because I knew what "going home" meant. My 81- year- old mother had died four years earlier. On my last visit with her, she pleaded to go home, for she had been suffering for years from alzheimer's disease. After her funeral I found a collection of quotes she had treasured. When I opened her notebook, I was comforted by the first quote I read. "To a Christian heaven is spelled HOME." I smiled to myself and thought, "You got your wish, Mom. Rest in peace."

Was Brandon telling me that he is going to die? Was something going to happen to him? I was restless all night as I tried to dismiss his words. The next morning I wrote the date of my " dream" on a calendar but did not tell anyone about it. Telling someone about the dream would make it "real." I could not deal with the possibility of those words coming true.

Story Two February 2003
I Know A Love

Children are not supposed to die before their parents. It just seems wrong. Brandon was my only child, and losing him would be the worst pain imaginable. I loved being a mom, and I looked forward to being a grandmother. I could not; I would not entertain the thought that Brandon might die. I still could not stop myself from having fearful thoughts that kept me awake night after night.

Two or three weeks after I had "the dream," I was at church. Kathy Dale Forrest, a choir member, sang a new song that she was recording for a CD. The song was entitled "I Know A Love." As I listened to the words, I felt overcome with chills. I thought to myself, "I want that song sung at my funeral." (Little did I know that this song would be sung a few weeks later, not for my funeral, but for Brandon's funeral.) The message of the song was about calming our fears in the dark and lonely hours of the night when we have endless questions and feel overwhelmed with hopelessness. It stressed that God loves us with a grace that is sufficient and that He is always near living within our hearts. I felt a resurgence of strength and faith because I trusted God to continue to make His Presence known to me. I was grateful that I knew His love.

THE PURPOSE DRIVEN LIFE

I was asked to lead a Lenten Bible study group at our church. In preparation for this study, I read <u>The Purpose Driven Life</u> by Rick Warren. It was an inspirational book that changed my perspective on life and gave me a clear understanding of what it means to live a life full of meaning and purpose. " It's NOT about ME" was the message emphasized in the book. I realized that our life on earth is temporary, and I am just passing through. My real home, my eternal home, is in heaven. That understanding reinforced and brought clarity to my mother's quote: "To the Christian, heaven is spelled HOME." Knowing our earthly death is not the end but the beginning gives us hope. Our death is our "birthday into heaven." (Little did I know at the time, that those words would bring me great comfort in the weeks to come.)

I am often reminded of a quote by Corrie ten Boom: "Every experience God gives us, every person He puts in our lives, is the perfect preparation for the future only He can see." God knew my future, and He was preparing me for Brandon's death. Brandon died four days after I led the first class. He was buried on a Monday morning, and I led the second class the following Tuesday night. The love and support from each person in my class was phenomenal. God had provided a grief support group for me before I knew that I would need one.

Three Days of Warning

I was a first- grade teacher. After breakfast one Monday morning, I was putting my coffee cup in the dish-washer. A terrible "thought" suddenly popped into my head. I thought, " Brandon's not going to live a long life." I was unnerved and scared. I tried my best to dismiss the thought, and I went to school. Twice that week the same thought popped into my mind during breakfast. I thought, "Okay, God, are You trying to tell me something?" Once again I did not tell anyone about what happened because telling someone would make it "real." I think I knew deep down that some-thing unimaginable could possibly happen, but I kept my faith. I put my trust in God to give me strength and peace as I hoped that everything would be okay.

THE KNOCK AT THE DOOR

I t was about 10:00 P.M. on a Friday night. I had already gone to bed and had just fallen asleep. I heard a knock at the door, but I did not get up. It was unusual for us to get company that late. A worried feeling overcame me. My husband opened the door, and then I heard a heart-wrenching cry. I knew immediately what had happened. I quickly dressed and went to see who was at our house. I was met by policemen, the coroner, and close friends with anguish on their faces. They had come to tell us that there had been an accident. I did not have to ask. I knew that Brandon had died and had gone "home". Everybody was surprised by my composure and lack of shock. I WAS devastated, but I also had a strange sense of calmness. God had been preparing me for this moment for several months. Looking back, I think He knew I would not have been able to bear the loss of my only child without His gentle intervention.

THE PURPLE IRISES

The funeral service for Brandon was beautiful. We were surrounded by family and many friends who showered us with their love and prayers. When Kathy Dale Forrest and the choir sang "I Know a Love," the song that had touched my heart a few weeks earlier, I felt God's grace surround me, and I felt a strength and a peace that surpasses all understanding, The words of the song were "So let the darkness come, it won't over-whelm my soul, My hope is in my God, and this I know." These words resonated in my heart and gave me the courage I needed to face our trip to the cemetery.

I asked my sister -in-law, Linda Quin, to pick some flowers from the cemetery and to take them to my house to make an arrangement. When I got home, I noticed a card on the counter from the Ardillo and Esteven families. On the card was a beautiful Siberian purple iris. The quote on the card by Thomas Moore read, "Earth has no sorrow that heaven can not heal." The words were profound and touched my heart. Sitting beside the card was a gift bag from Donna Knapp. It was filled with several books about grief . On the bag was another big, beautiful purple iris. I turned around and saw the vase of flowers my sister-in-law had made from the flowers at the cemetery. In the vase there were three beautiful purple irises just like the ones on the card and the gift bag. An idea just popped into my head. I thought, " The purple iris is going to be my Brandon flower." That was no coincidence. It was a God-incidence.

Making the purple iris my Brandon flower was the beginning of a journey that has lasted for over fourteen years. For fourteen years God has comforted me with purple irises everywhere I go. God speaks to me through nature in many creative, joyful ways. From Louisiana, Tennessee, and California to Hawaii and Alaska and many other places, the purple iris has comforted me and brought me joy. Every time I see one, I am thankful for God and Brandon being with me.

When I googled the meaning of the Siberian purple iris, I learned that it is a symbol of faith, wisdom, and hope. The Egyptians used the iris to symbolize their connections to heaven.

THE YELLOW BUTTERFLY

A couple of days after Brandon's funeral, I was restless and felt that I needed to get out and be alone. It was spring, and the flowers were beautiful. I decided to ride to a nursery in Baton Rouge. The idea that the purple iris would be my Brandon flower was in the back of my mind. I was just rambling around Clegg's Nursery when I suddenly saw a stepping stone plaque hanging on the wall. I froze and felt an overwhelming warmth and excitement when I realized that the plaque had a cross and purple irises on it. The plaque was a gift from heaven telling me that Brandon and God were looking out for me and wanted to comfort me. Of course, I bought the plaque.

I took the plaque to show my pastor, Reverend Bill Willis. I was excited to show him the purple irises and to tell him my story. He noticed something that I had not. Over the irises was a yellow butterfly. Reverend Willis reminded me that the butterfly is a symbol of the resurrection, hope, and reassurance of life after death. I knew then that God would nourish me and give me more beautiful experiences of His Presence in my life to help me get through the grief process and survive the loss of my child.

Soon after visiting my pastor, I read a story about a group of grieving caterpillars. The caterpillars were carrying a dead cocoon to its final resting place. The caterpillars were heartbroken and crying. Their heads hung low in grief. If the caterpillars had been looking up, they would have seen the beautiful butterfly fluttering above. It was a beautiful story and inspired me to make the yellow butterfly another symbol of God's grace and Brandon's nearness in my life. I was reminded to look up and to think of Brandon in heaven, not to look down and think of his grave. He is alive living in his heavenly home. The scripture from Colossians 3:2 reminds me to "set your mind on things above, not on things of the earth."

WHEN WE ASK WHY

My good friend, Ursula Sherman, was convinced she had a poem for me. A nun had given her the poem at her husband's funeral many years ago. She decided she would frame the poem with a picture of a purple iris. I happened to have the perfect picture from an Easter card I had gotten at Winn Dixie. Ursula took the card to scan the picture to go with her poem.

Ursula usually got her oil changed in her car in Amite. For some reason, she decided to go to Hammond. She stopped at Fastlane, a place she had never been before. While waiting for her oil to be changed , she saw a rack filled with greeting cards. She was astounded when she saw a purple iris and a yellow butterfly on a card. The words " When We Ask Why" were on the front of the card. She read the poem inside the card and immediately knew that THAT poem was the poem God had meant for me. God had brought her to this place to discover that card. She hurried home and called me.

When Ursula arrived at my house, I saw excitement radiating from her face. I felt God's love and grace surround me as I read the poem "When We Ask Why." The words, emotions, and thoughts expressed in the poem mirrored explicitly conversations Ursula and I had in the weeks following Brandon's death. We had talked about how bad things happen to good people and how there were tragedies in life that could not be explained. We had talked about our faith and trusted that God had a plan and a purpose for our lives. We did not understand the "why" of many things, but we knew we needed to trust in God's wisdom.

I asked Ursula to show me the poem that had meant so much to her. It was entitled "Tapestry." The words of that poem gave me a deeper understanding and perspective about how to view the dark times in my life. The analogy of thinking of my entire life as a tapestry with dark threads for the times of sorrow and bright, beautiful colors for times of joy was profound. I was thankful Ursula shared both poems with me. They each helped me to try to see life from God's perspective and further encouraged me to walk by faith and trust that God would always be with me.

When We Ask Why

God's beautiful plan
Is sometimes concealed,
But someday His purpose
Will be fully revealed.

Someday God's wisdom
Will make it very plain
Why problems were permitted
And how He uses pain.

Things thought illogical—
Disease, tragedy, fear—
Will someday make sense
When God makes all things clear.

We'll see the Lord's purpose
From Heaven's point of view,
And we will understand
In ways we never knew.

Till we are home with God
Some answers have to wait.
"Lord, we'll TRUST AND OBEY.
Lord, help us walk by faith".

21

When We Ask Why

God's beautiful plan
Is sometimes concealed,
But someday His purpose
Will be fully revealed.

Someday God's wisdom
Will make it very plain
Why problems were permitted
And how He uses pain.

Things thought illogical-
Disease, tragedy, fear-
Will someday make sense
When God makes all things clear.

We'll see the Lord's purpose
From Heaven's point of view,
And we will understand
In ways we never knew.

Till we are home with God
Some answers have to wait
"Lord, we'll TRUST and OBEY.
Lord, help us walk by faith".
Perry Tankeley

TAPESTRY

My life is but a weaving between God and me.
I do not choose the colors; He worketh steadily.
Oft times He weaves sorrow, and I in foolish pride,
forget He sees the upper, and I the underside.
Not 'til the loom is silent and shuttles cease to fly,
will God unroll the canvas and explain the
reason why.
The dark threads are as needful in the skillful
Weaver's Hand, as the threads of gold and silver
in the pattern He has planned.
AUTHOR UNKNOWN

The First Mother's Day

I had really been dreading Mother's Day without Brandon. The week before Mother's Day was the hardest time that I had had since his death. I decided to go to church to teach my adult Sunday School class, but I knew that I could not make myself stay for the church service. I was too uncomfortable and self- conscious because I knew that everyone would feel sorry for me. I knew that the pastor would ask all mothers to stand up to receive a flower. Did I stand up or not? Was I still a mother? I could not put myself through the torture, and I was certain that God would understand. I did not want to see or talk to anyone. It would be too painful to hear people wishing everyone a "Happy Mother's Day!"

Instead of going to church, my husband and I rode to New Orleans. As I was walking through the Lakeside Mall, I stopped at a little shop displaying bracelets. I was mindlessly flipping through the bracelets when I saw my Mother's Day gift. For a little while, I was excited and energized that God had led me to find a bracelet made with colorful "butterflies." The bracelet helped me keep my focus on God by giving me strength to get through the day. How little did I know that the best was yet to come!

We then left Lakeside Mall and went to Esplanade Mall. Walking through the upper level, I could see booths set up everywhere, for people were selling Mother's Day gifts. From a distance I saw some plaques with purple irises painted on them. I HAD to take a closer look. The first plaque said " To My Grandmother." "Oh well," I thought, "not for me." I took a few more steps, caught my breath, and read, "To My Mother." As I read the poem, the tears began to fall again. The words were perfect. They were just what Brandon would have said if he were alive. I KNEW it was his gift to me, and I was overjoyed with a thankful heart. Running through the mall with the plaque in my hands and tears running down my face, I met my husband. I could not wait to show him what Brandon had given me for Mother's Day. I was going to survive the day after all.

When I got home, I could not wait to show my friend Ursula. She could not believe the plaque. She said that she had prayed that morning that Brandon would speak to me in some special way on this Mother's Day. What an awesome answer to a prayer from this special Christian friend!

To My Mother

All my life, I've been able
To count on you-
to listen, to understand, to love me,
even at my most unlovable-
You're the kind of mother
other mothers strive to be;
and I feel lucky you're mine
So, though I may not tell you
as often as I should'
don't ever think for a moment
that I don't appreciate you..
Because-as far as I'm concerned-
you're the best there is.

I love you

A DRAGONFLY WILL DO

It had been four months since Brandon's death. Reality of not seeing Brandon again on earth had set in, and I cried a lot. I was thankful that I had been blessed to have Brandon in my life for twenty- six years, but I just missed him. As tears rolled down my cheeks, I was telling God that He knew best and that His grace, comfort, and strength had been more than I could have asked for. Then I felt peace in knowing that Brandon was in heaven and that he had no pain, worry , or problems. I was just really sad.

I decided to ride to Ponchatoula to a restaurant called Stricks. Brandon had talked about this place all the time. He would say, "Mom, they have the best seafood stuffed potatoes!" I decided that I would go there , in his honor, and get something to eat. BIG mistake! I cried the whole time I was in there. It was a busy time, and quite a few people were in line in front of me. Tears rolled down my cheeks as I stood in line. When I finally got to the front to place my order, I was a mess. The owner greeted me. Misinterpreting my facial expression, the man said, "Ma'am, I'm sorry you had to wait so long." I was a basket case as I tried to say, "I'm not crying because I had to wait. I am crying because my son liked to eat here, and he died."

The poor fellow did not know what to do or say. I went on to tell him the story about Brandon. He remembered Brandon and said that he had done business with him when Brandon worked with a finance company in Ponchatoula. He was complimentary of the business relationship they had had.

I finally placed my order. I should have left, but I was determined that I was going to get that stuffed potato. When the order arrived, I went to pay for it, but they insisted that it was "on the house". I think they saw my tears and just wanted to get me out of there.

I got the order to go. As I was driving home, I could smell how good the food was. I thought to myself, "I really ought to eat the potato while it is hot." I was literally crying and laughing at the same time as I thought about how ridiculous the situation was. I could sense Brandon laughing at me and telling me to pull over and eat. I pulled into the parking lot near a dollar store. It was hot, so I put the windows down. Eating with tears falling was not the most appetizing of meals, but I was determined.

As I sat there thinking how funny this story would be one day, I said to God, "This would be a good time for a butterfly to visit." I knew that God was not a genie in the sky and did not answer requests on demand, but a butterfly surely would have been appreciated. No butterfly came. A few minutes later I looked up, and there were several dragonflies on my windshield. I fell out laughing and said, "Thank you, God, "A dragonfly will do! "

At the time I had no idea that in the future the dragonfly would become a recurring visitor as a symbol of God's presence and guidance.

MOUNTAIN TOP EXPERIENCES

I was in Pigeon Forge, Tennessee, staying in a mountain top chateau named "Eagle's Wings." I was sitting in a rocking chair on the back porch of the cabin watching the sun rise over the mountains. It was a beautiful fall morning, and I was crying. I seldom indulged myself in a crying spell, for I was a champion at suppressing my tears. But on that particular morning, I needed to let the tears of sadness and loss flow as I had a good talk with God.

That morning God revealed Himself to me through nature. As I looked up at the sky, I saw the sign of the cross. It looked as though two jets had crossed, but there were no jets around. As I looked at the cross, I thought about how much God loved us. He sent His Son Jesus to die on the cross for our sins. I thought of the sinful person I was and the sins Brandon had had. I was thankful that God would forgive us both and welcome us into heaven with open, loving arms. As I continued to look at the cross, the bottom began to disappear, and I noticed a skinny, fluffy upward line of clouds going toward heaven. It revealed to me a visible sign that the cross leads to heaven. It was as if God and Brandon were telling me where he was. I cried tears of joy, thankfulness, and heartache at the same time. It was a beautiful experience. I could feel Brandon's spirit with me.

After experiencing the cross in the sky, I opened Upper Room, a daily devotional book I often read. Coincidentally (no way), the prayer focus that morning was "Someone Facing Great Loss." The last paragraph stressed that when experiencing a tragedy, we can trust in God who will never leave or forsake us.

I asked God how He wanted me to use my pain, loss, and experience to help others in similar circumstances. I asked how I could be a "light" for Him and how I could direct others to Him. Half an hour later, I read another daily devotional, In Touch by Charles Stanley. Why was I not surprised that the devotional was talking about bringing others along on this journey with me? It said that I needed to help others make this journey. How much more validation did I need? Just what I was thinking about was what the daily devotional was talking about. God was truly at work in the world around me with the devotionals I read that morning. He was telling me to help others just as He was helping me. I was to share the strength, the courage, hope, and the peace that comes only from a living faith and trust in God's love and grace.

As I was writing my thoughts and feelings in a journal, two eagles flew overhead. They reminded me of the scripture from Isaiah 40:31: "They that wait upon the Lord shall renew their strength, they shall mount up as wings with eagles; they shall run, and not be weary; and they shall walk and not faint." I knew that God was my strength. When I booked the cabin that we were staying in, I had no idea that the name "On Eagle's Wings" would have such meaning, (God knew where He wanted me to be to hear His message bright and clear.)

Another book I was rereading at the time was The Purpose Driven Life by Rick Warren. On that particular morning, I was journaling on the back pages of this book. I was seeking serious guidance and strength about how to surrender my pain to God and how to renew a sense of purpose in my life. In his book Rick Warren suggests that we pray this prayer to God in heaven: "Father, if this problem, pain, sickness, or cir-cumstance is needed to fulfill your purpose and glory in my life or in another's , please don't take it away. " He says that the blessings of surrender are peace, freedom, and God's power. I knew that God was speaking to me in a powerful way that morning. His message was heard and received.

BRANDON'S FIRST BIRTHDAY – PART 1

THE GIFT OF JOY

In anticipation of Brandon's birthday and my first celebration without him, I was struggling and trying hard not to be depressed. By nature I am a positive and upbeat person. For some reason, I felt guilty for wanting to be happy, for being able to laugh, and for trying to live with a joyful heart. I felt that I was betraying my child if I started to feel joy again. This guilt had been weighing heavily on my heart for weeks.

On the day before Brandon's birthday, I was walking around a Christian bookstore in Baton Rouge. A framed picture of a purple iris caught my eye. The scripture on the picture was from Philippians 4:4. It said , "Rejoice in the Lord always." I thought to myself, "How am I supposed to have joy when my child has died, and I can not be with him on his birthday?" I took a few more steps around a corner, and there was another picture with a lavender colored iris . The picture had the second part of the above scripture with these words:"And again I say rejoice!" Wow! That got my attention. I realized that God was trying to tell me something powerful. Even though I had suffered a great loss, He was encouraging me to seek and accept "joy" in my life. Needless to say, I bought both pictures.

When I started the car to drive home, a song by Kathy Dale Forrest was playing on the CD player. Kathy Dale was the person who sang " I Know A Love" at Brandon's funeral. The first words I heard were "Rejoice, rejoice, and again I say rejoice!" God must have really thought I was hard-headed, and I appreciated His effort to make sure that I had heard His message. My heart was softening to the possibility of being able to experience true joy again.

Things seemed to happen to me "in threes." When I got home, I decided to look at my God Calling book. My friend, Frances Catalanotto , taught me to randomly open the book. She assured me that I would discover the message God wanted me to hear. I followed her instructions, and surely enough, for the third time, God was telling me that I should "rejoice" more even in the daily struggles along life's way. Nehemiah 8:10 states: "The joy of the Lord is my strength."

Story Thirteen November 2003
BRANDON'S FIRST BIRTHDAY - PART 2
THE BRANDON GARDEN

Brandon's first birthday finally arrived. I was glad; I wanted to "get it over." I was emotionally drained from the anticipation of it. I decided to make a "Brandon Garden" in my front yard. Once again I drove to Clegg's Nursery in Baton Rouge. As I was walking around looking at all the plants, a yellow butterfly began to flutter around me. (I am not kidding.) The butterfly kept landing on some beautiful red azalea bushes. I felt that the butterfly was leading me to the plants Brandon would like in his garden. I was excited as I felt his presence guiding me.

The MOST exciting thing happened next. As I was driving home, I was thinking about Brandon's birthday and wondering if he was having a happy birthday in heaven. When I drove around a big curve, I saw a sign, a REAL SIGN, a really big sign, high in the air. The sign was on a billboard in front of a little country church. I was blown away when I read the message on the sign. I thanked God for his imaginative ways of speaking to me. The sign read, "Happiness is in heaven, but there is JOY in the journey." That was the perfect message for me, for it validated that Brandon was indeed in heaven and that it was okay for me to have "JOY" in my journey while still on earth. I was the one who received a gift on Brandon's birthday....the "gift of joy!"

To add "icing to the cake," that afternoon a yellow butterfly fluttered around and kept me company as I planted the azalea bushes in my new "Brandon Garden."

Brandon's First Birthday – Part 3
Christiana's Visit and Dream

I t was Brandon's first birthday after his death. I would not be spending his birthday with him. I knew I needed to be strong. I read a daily devotional written by Charles Stanley in <u>In Touch.</u> The lesson that day was about strength (another God-incidence). The lesson stated that we would be strong because God would be strong in us. It is God's presence, strength, and ability living in us that is manifested through us. I desperately wanted to live in God's strength and be a witness to His overwhelming love and grace that had surrounded me for the last nine months. God had been my refuge and my strength. I wanted to reflect God's light to everyone around me and to be a living witness to His power in a grieving mother's life.

On the day before Brandon's birthday, which was a Sunday, my church family and close friends did their best to cheer me with their company and thoughtful gifts. On that day I needed some quiet time. Only one yellow butterfly visited me in my backyard.

My niece, Christiana Quin Wharton, and her baby girl Tinley surprised me with a visit. She had the perfect and most thoughtful gift for me. How she found it, I did not know. (God really made me smile with His creative thinking!) It was a purse, and I love purses. But THIS purse was decorated with what looked like hand-painted irises and butterflies.

Christiana proceeded to tell me about a dream that she had had on the night Brandon died. She had waited until this day to share the dream with me. She said that Brandon had come to her in a dream. He had been waiting for her and Jason, her husband, to get to the funeral home on the night of his wake. He told her that he could not "go" until he had talked to her and asked her to take care of my husband and me. He said that he could go "in peace" if he knew we would be okay. I thought that was so sweet. We cried bittersweet tears. Christiana's true gift to me was not the purse. It was "the dream."

Through Christiana, Brandon had a special message for me on his birthday. I called to tell Ursula, my friend, about Christiana's visit. Later that day, Ursula called to tell me she had just read in a Christian book "Don't take dreams lightly." How's that for a God-incidence?

THE FIRST CHRISTMAS (FROM MY JOURNAL)

BUTTERFLIES AND PURPLE IRISES

It was too hard to stay home for Christmas. I could not pretend to be happy around everyone so that no one would feel sorry for me. I wanted to be alone. Susan Jenkins, a sweet friend, came to see me. Susan had just returned from Calloway Gardens in Pine Mountain, Georgia. She knew all about my "butterfly stories." She told me that there was a huge butterfly conservatory in Pine Mountain, and it was amazing. Visiting the conservatory sounded like a good idea. Unfortunately, I learned it was a popular destination place at Christmas time, and it would be almost impossible to get reservations.

The week before Christmas I decided to take a chance and call for reservations. I knew that getting a reservation was doubtful, but I felt that this was the perfect place for my husband and me to go. No one would know us, and I would not have to pretend that I was not heartbroken. After Brandon died, I had learned that trying not to cry was exhausting. I would not have had the strength to hold back tears if I had stayed home and celebrated with my family. My family understood.

When I called Calloway Gardens Inn, I found that there had been a cancellation. Considering how God had blessed me in such delightful ways, I really was not surprised that I was able to get a reservation for Christmas.

To say that this trip was just what I needed was an understatement. Walking around the butterfly conservatory with beautiful butterflies literally flying around everywhere was an emotional, yet comforting experience. It was a tangible, visible demonstration of God's love and grace. It reminded me of Colossians 3:2 : "Set your mind on things above, not on things of the earth." The butterflies constantly reminded me to look up and keep my focus on God.

A recurring theme at Christmas time is that God gives us Christ, the Light of the world, to bring us hope. Christmas is supposed to be a time of joy and celebration, but for many it can be a season of darkness and sorrow. It is easy to succumb to a feeling of darkness when experiencing the grief and loss of a child or anyone close to you for that matter. I was fighting the feeling of darkness.

One of the special Christmas events in the Pine Mountain area was called "The Festival of the Lights." It was an hour- long trolley ride through a forest that had Christmas-themed decorated lights. I needed "light" to cheer me up. I clearly remember riding the trolley with tears in my eyes. I did not want to embarrass myself by bursting into tears, so I silently chanted to myself, "Jesus is the Light. Jesus is the Light. Jesus is the Light....." My first surprise was when we entered the area of brightly lit yellow butterflies. I felt the" light" of God's love deep in my heart. Near the end of the tour, I was astounded to see the flower area with a beautiful purple iris shining brightly. I found my "light in the darkness" that night.

It was Christmas Eve, and I was still basking in the glow of my "Fantasy in the Lights" experience. Although I was trying very hard to fight it , the darkness that comes with grief was beginning to settle over me like a dark cloud. Just to pass time, I went to a mall nearby. I was not looking for anything in particular. By chance (or a God-incident), I walked into a store that was jam-packed with so many items that I could barely walk around. Then I saw SOMETHING on a shelf in a corner. Was that what I thought it was? Did it have on it what I thought it did? I was mesmerized as I walked closer to check it out. God would "hit the ball out of the ballpark" with this surprise if it was what I thought it was. It was the ultimate Christmas gift! I saw a light, a lamp light. On the sides of the lamp were butterflies and irises. I could not believe that I had found a "light" that would shine with butterflies and irises. It reminded me of the scripture from John 8:12. Jesus says , " I am the light of the world; whoever follows me will never walk in darkness, but will have the light of life."

Merry Christmas to me! I was filled with joy and the "light of Christ!"

LESSONS LEARNED THROUGH GRIEF

It was New Year's Eve 2003. I was sitting in Brandon's bedroom thinking about how much I missed him. The only way I could get through Christmas was by thinking that Brandon had spent Christmas with Jesus. Knowing that he was happy and at peace helped me to accept life without him. I really do not think of Brandon being dead. I think of him living somewhere else now. I know one day I will see him again in heaven.

God had been so merciful and kind in the months following Brandon's death. He did so many things to uplift my spirit and to assure me that I was not alone. I thanked God for His grace, for it was His grace that enabled me to see Him at work in the world around me through the people supporting me and through nature. I knew that God was in control and that He wanted me to grow in spiritual maturity, understanding, and knowledge of His love through the tragedy I had experienced.

God taught me that in my weakness He would make me strong. I learned to surrender myself to His will and trust that He would provide the comfort, peace, perseverance, and strength I needed not only to endure but also to live a life of joy. That is something I would never have thought possible. I understood then how God had prepared me for the greatest heartbreak of my life. I thought of a quote by Corrie ten Boom: "Every experience God gives us, every person He puts in our lives, is the perfect preparation for the future that only He can see."

I learned that suffering does produce perseverance and endurance when I trust that God will hold my hand through each day. I just wish that I could have learned "the peace that surpasses all understanding" without having to have lost my son. Even though 2003 was a heartbreaking year, I grew closer to God than I had ever been. I learned "The joy of the Lord is my strength" (Nehemiah 8:10).

I accepted the fact that I would love Brandon forever and that I would miss him forever, but I also made a decision to keep living, loving, and laughing as Brandon would have wanted. Even though I did not know what the New Year would bring, I decided to choose to trust God knowing He would never leave me. I chose to begin the New Year with hope and a grateful heart. Jeremiah

19:11 says, "I know I have plans for you," says the Lord, "plans to prosper you and not harm you, plans to give you hope and a future."

ONE YEAR LATER

I could not believe that it had been a year since Brandon died. The past twelve months seemed to have passed like a blur in my mind. It made me see "time" differently. One year is nothing; neither are five or twenty years. They all pass so quickly. I realized that our time on earth is limited, but I was comforted in knowing that I would have eternity to live with Brandon when I saw him again in heaven.

Before Brandon died, I had read <u>The Purpose Driven Life</u> by Rick Warren. As a result, I was able to deal with the tragedy of his death in a much different way. The book helped me to focus not on myself and on my feelings but to look through the darkness and to see God's light. I knew that I did not have the strength to survive after losing my son on my own. I sought God's presence through prayer, through scriptures, through devotionals, and through Christian books on grief and joy, as well as through counsel and support from loving friends and family.

I knew that God wanted me to use my experiences to share His light, His strength, and His promises with others who had lost a loved one. I felt God wanted me to show others how to continue to give glory, honor, and praise to Him . He had carried me through my loss and grief. He had filled me with an attitude of joy and peace that would have been impossible without His love and grace. Sometimes I felt guilty for being able to handle my grief so well. I realized it was not about me at all; it was all about God's Holy Spirit living within me. " For God has not given us the spirit of fear, but of power, and of love, and of a sound mind" (2 Timothy 1:7).

I was at peace with God, and I knew Brandon was happy. Both God and Brandon had sent me many signs to prove that they were with me. The yellow butterfly that appeared so many times and in so many places as we traveled around the country reminded me of Brandon's "new life in Christ" and to always "look up" and keep my focus on God. The purple irises I saw everywhere were God's way of communicating to me that He and Brandon were near in spirit. I felt their love and presence which gave me comfort and the peace that surpasses all understanding.

Kirk Hood, a special friend, had ordered a variety of purple iris bulbs for me to plant in my Brandon

Garden. I planted the bulbs in January with the hope that they would bloom to celebrate Brandon's first year in heaven. My heart was joy-filled when I went outside to see the beautiful flowers in his garden on his first birthday in heaven! Later that afternoon I looked out my window and saw two yellow butterflies fluttering around the garden. I smiled and said, "Thank you, God!" and "Happy Birthday in heaven, Brandon!"

A DRAGONFLY WILL DO – PART 2

In June 2016, Hoppie, my husband, had open-heart surgery. Whenever I got stir-crazy from sitting in his hospital room too long, I would walk down the halls and look at the artwork. On one particular trip, I decided to take a different route. I saw a beautiful painting of purple irises. I thanked God for guiding me to that picture and felt His presence and Brandon's presence giving me encouragement and hope.

After a successful surgery and three nights in the hospital, we went home. The next morning Hoppie had to be rushed back to the hospital in an ambulance. He was in great pain. I tried to be strong as I followed the ambulance to Covington. I knew that God was in control. I trusted in His grace and knew that everything would be okay.

During our second stay at the hospital, I saw several different paintings of purple irises but never any yellow butterflies. I needed a butterfly to remind me to look up and keep my focus on God. I needed His strength, His courage, and His peace to help me take care of Hoppie. I knew that He would give me the hope and the assurance I needed to know that Hoppie would recover and not leave me as Brandon did.

I decided to check my Facebook page and update my friends on Hoppie's progress. I was surprised and delighted when I saw the first post on my page. It was a video entitled "Dragonfly Convention." I was reminded of a time thirteen years earlier when I asked God to send a yellow butterfly to comfort me. God had a different plan, a better plan. He sent a dragonfly. He knew the dragonfly was a symbol of hope and His presence. I smiled and thought once again, "A Dragonfly Will Do!"

The
Dragonfly

In wonder I watch the
dragonflies dance over
the water, wings so light
and transparent held up
by the wind .. like we are
held up by the cross

A Time to Write & A Time to Soar

When Brandon died, I was in my thirty-second year of teaching first- grade at Amite Elementary. A year later I retired. The next year I started working for a textbook publishing company with Donna Knapp, a close friend. We traveled a lot. I missed being at home so I retired from that job. I remembered how much I loved teaching and being with young children, so I took a position teaching kindergarten at Oak Forest Academy, a small private school near my home. I taught for three years. I then worked with the teachers and the students for seven more years. My years at Oak Forest Academy were a balm to my soul.

I finally retired, for the third time, in 2014. Although my husband and I did a lot of traveling, I had more time to spend at home. Writing a book became a possibility.

I knew I had to write the book in God's time, so I waited for a sign or revelation to encourage me to get started.

As I read back through fourteen years of journal writings, I was reminded of a few incidences where a dragonfly was involved. My favorite story was the time I asked God to send a butterfly to cheer me up, and He sent a dragonfly instead. I remembered how God's sense of humor had made me laugh. It was then that I got the idea for the title of this book : "A Dragonfly Will Do." I thought it would be a catchy title and provoke curiosity in the reader.

In one of my journals, I wrote about finding a Christmas ornament shaped like a cross with a dragonfly on it. When I read the message attached to the cross, I felt God urging me to buy the cross. The message said, "In wonder I watch the dragonflies dance over the water, wings so light and transparent held up by the wind...like we are held up by the cross." God was planting a "seed" in my mind. The seed grew each time I saw another dragonfly.

In June 2007, I started to notice dragonflies in my back yard. I googled "dragonfly" and was intrigued and fascinated by what I discovered. " Legend has it that dragonflies were given an extra set of wings so that angels could ride on their back, smaller than small, yet whenever you see a winged masterpiece , you can be certain that an angel has come down from heaven to visit you. The dragonfly's appearance was to remind us that even though we are apart from our loved ones, their spirit was always with us in our hearts." Reading about dragonflies inspired me. Through the dragonfly sightings, I felt God was sending me the message that the time to write had arrived.

During the second week of June 2007, we went to San Francisco, California. I had dragonflies on my mind. In a shop at Pier 39 , I found a beautiful drag-onfly necklace. As I browsed in a shop in Sausalito , I told the owner that I was looking for something with a dragonfly. He immediately went to a glass display filled with necklaces. He showed me a dragonfly necklace that resembled a locket. The dragonfly locket opened and inside was a magnifying glass. What message did God have for me? Was God telling me that I should magnify His glory in my book? I bought the necklace hoping that God would help me to see the "bigger picture" and to see more clearly the path He had set before me. I went home with two dragonfly necklaces, a bracelet, several pairs of earrings, and a lapel pen. I was in "dragonfly overload" and ready to write.

My last purchase was a cute little dragonfly charm. Attached to the charm was a message meant especially for me. I thought that the message would be a good ending for this book: "Always have faith, be true to you. Enjoy the journey and love what you do. Share your blessings, live simply each day. Let your spirit soar, and good will come your way."

A Time to Give Thanks

Scripture states that there is a time for everything: "There is a time to be born and a time to die. There is a time to weep and a time to laugh" (Ecclesiastes 3). I think there is a time for butterflies and a time for dragonflies.

I recently saw a cartoon about a young child who asked, "Do caterpillars know they're going to be butterflies, or does God surprise them?" I think that God likes to surprise us. He has certainly surprised me in the most delightful and joyful ways with butterflies, purple irises, and dragonflies. I am extremely thankful for God's sense of humor which He has demonstrated by sending dragonflies to inspire me to write this book.

I am thankful that God keeps His promises. "The Lord is my refuge and my strength, and a very present help in time of trouble" (Psalm 46:1). In First Thessalonians 5:18, the Bible tells us " to give thanks in all circumstances, for this is God's will for you in Christ Jesus." I now understand that God did not expect me to be thankful FOR my circumstance, but He did expect me to be thankful IN this circumstance knowing that His love, care, peace, and wisdom would carry me through my grief process.

Thank you, Ursula Sherman, my friend and editor. When I doubted myself, you gave me the encouragement that I needed to keep writing. Through more than three decades of good times and bad times, your friendship, guidance, prayers, and love have been a meaningful support to me. I treasure our friendship.

Thank you, Baylee Smith , for being my technology expert. When I asked for your help, your first words were, " Yes, it's a 'God thing' that you asked me this week because I will be gone to college next week". God's timing, as usual, is always perfect.

The saying "Friends are angels who lift you up when you believe your wings have forgotten how to fly" is true. I am thankful for the "angels" in my life. On the night Brandon died, my "angels" appeared. Arriving with the policemen and coroner to tell my husband and me about the accident were Kirk and Bill Hood. I think my first hug came from Kirk. Thank you, Kirk, for your never-ending love and support. Thank you to all our friends that came that night to offer their love and support. When Glenn Hutchinson asked me what he could do to help, I remember saying, "Go to Kentwood and get Brandon's two dogs and five two-week old puppies." It was good he was a vet so that he could handle the challenge. We had puppies at our house within a few hours. Thank you, Glenn. The puppies gave us something to smile about.

On our trip to the cemetery after Brandon's funeral, we were blessed to have Kirk and Bill Hood and Peggy and Mike Scarle ride with us. Thank you, Bill and Mike, for loving Brandon like a son. Your company and conversation on that trip to Kentwood helped us to prepare for our final good-bye. I can still see Kay, Libby, Frances, Ursula, Ramona, Lindy, Lana and Sonja sitting at my kitchen table many times with love in their eyes and words of encouragement. They should all win an award for all the butterfly and purple iris cards and novelty items they found to bring me. They were most assuredly vessels through whom God worked to bless and strengthen my spirit.

My church family at the First United Methodist Church of Amite surrounded my husband and me with their loving arms. The members of the Lenten Bible study I was leading at the time of Brandon's death became my grief support team, and the adult Sunday School class I was teaching became "angels" in my eyes with their prayers and support. A church member and former classmate of my husband's, Martha Alexander , painted us a beautiful picture of three purple irises and a butterfly. She told my husband that the butterfly was more orange and blue than yellow because those were the colors of their high school alma mater, Kentwood High School.

When I went back to teaching the week after Brandon's funeral, my principal and friend, Libby Covington, welcomed me with open arms. She checked on me several times a day and would always say, " Now if you need to go home, it's okay. I'll get someone to teach your class." I did not want to leave my classroom and see people. I knew that they felt sorry for me and would be at a loss for words. Ramona LaBarbera, a close friend and fellow teacher, insisted that she take my class with hers to the lunchroom and bring them back after lunch. It was so hard for me to accept help, but Ramona's offer was the most thoughtful gift. I graciously accepted.

I want to thank the children in my first- grade class of 2003. Being at school with them brought a "light into my darkness." They made me laugh, and for a short while each day, they made me forget my pain. Ursula's grand daughter, Mallory, was in my class that year. When Mallory went home from school one day, she told Ursula "Miss Beverly had a bad day at school today." When Ursula asked what had happened, Mallory said, "She was teaching with tears falling down her cheeks. She would turn her head so we couldn't see, but I did." My sweet little six- year- olds were filled with compassion and cared for me. The class gave me a big statue of a little boy petting two little puppies. When I look at the statue in my Brandon Garden, I think of the precious children in my class of 2003.

When I retired the following year, Libby gave me a special retirement gift. It was a cross necklace intertwined with a Siberian purple iris. The necklace was an heirloom from her mother, Sarah Falcon. I know that Miss Sarah and Brandon still smile in heaven whenever I wear the necklace. Thank you, Lib, for that priceless gift.

A special thank you goes to a former first-grade student of mine from Amite Elementary. I taught Nikki Falcone in 1992. After Brandon died, she wrote me a letter telling me how I had inspired her to become a first- grade teacher. In the last paragraph of her letter she wrote, "I hope this letter brightens your day, and though your biological son is gone, you have many children, and I feel privileged to be one." Thank you Nikki, for helping me realize that even though I did not have a living legacy through my child, I did have all the children that I was blessed to teach for forty years.

Losing Brandon was hard enough, but to "add salt to the wound" was the thought of never being a grandmother. Sadly, in 2005, my brother, Billy Quin, died. Only seven months earlier Billy's wife had died. That meant that Billy and Donna's children would have no grandparents on the Quin side. Hoppie and I were blessed with the opportunity to become "MiMi and Popa Hop" to six "grandchildren" born after Brandon died. It astounds me the way God works things out to give His children what they need. My brother and I swapped families. My brother is in heaven with Brandon, and I am here on earth with his children. I am blessed with the joy of being a grandmother after all !

Through the words, thoughtful gestures, prayers, and actions of the people mentioned in this book, as well as many unnamed saints, I hope you will understand how God works in the world around us. God showed His love and Presence through many people. God also showed me His love and Presence through nature. I am inspired by this quote from George Washington Carver: "I love to think of nature as an unlimited broadcasting station, through which God speaks to us every hour, if we will only tune in." Using the purple iris, the yellow butterfly, and the dragonfly, God gave me comfort, encouragement, strength, peace, and JOY. I am humbled by the tangible, visible, and amazing ways God showed His love for me. Before I would start writing stories for this book, I would pray, " Lord, bless this book and the stories written so that those who read the book will be blessed and will better understand how You work in the world around us when we look for Your Presence with 'eyes of faith.' "

CPSIA information can be obtained
at www.ICGtesting.com
Printed in the USA
LVOW07s1245091017
551752LV00011B/1226/P

9 781545 613344